Memories in Clay, Dreams of Wolves

Memories in Clay, Dreams of Wolves

Matthew
All the best!

Poems
by David Anthony Sam

Published by Create Space

Publication Data

Sam, David Anthony, 1949-

Memories in Clay, Dreams of Wolves ; poems / by David
Anthony Sam – 1st ed.

ISBN-13: 978-1496078834

ISBN-10: 1496078837

Cover art by Cynthia Ann Price
Cover design and Photo of Author by Ryan W. Mitchell

Manufactured in the United States of America
Published May 15, 2014

Dedication

To Linda,
without whom so much has less meaning.

Under the trellis
of snow and bright lights
where summer flowers had bloomed,
with words that turned visible
in the cold December air,
you became my forever.

Table of Contents

"We are known forever by the tracks we leave behind."

Dakota Proverb

"Nature teaches more than she preaches. There are no sermons in stones. It is easier to get a spark out of a stone than a moral."

John Burroughs

Prologue

The Songs Between

There are certain places, certain times
when the soul flies freely
and feels one with the wind,
and one with the land,
and one with the lives around it.

I have been graced with such places,
such moments. They have demanded
with need that I voice them
and allowed my voice to fulfill them.

A Wyoming prairie sings to me.
A cold lake in Oregon
made fresh from old winter snow dying.
A lakeshore where waves clap,
or an ocean of sand beside
an ocean of sea and mist.

A small room with her face.
A park with their laughter.
A mountainside made blue to me by distance,
and a wide river valley between
full of green, a gray slab of road,
and the brown winding river.

There are such places, such times
that make me think if death were this–
this open disappearing into life–
death would be a fine thing.

Instead I live between such places
and such moments waiting only.

And the song finds me when I am ready.

Fatherhood

There was the valley,
the Youghiogheny cutting
through rounded mountains,
the red clay my father dug
with pickax and shovel
to force a home from
the grudging hillside.

The time was new, the clay
dark red with iron,
the wind warm enough
for summer, but not so
hot you'd think of death.
My father grunted with
each heft and swing.

He sculpted that clay
with the same careful
touch he used when he
etched our busts in
redwood. He showed me
the meaning of the red clay,
the river in the valley

cleft, the rounded mountains.
He showed me the tracks
of the deer, the shy brown
flash of doe between
green undergrowth. He
showed me how to find
wild onions by their

leaves, and how to
recognize wild cherry
trees by their black
bark and sweet sap.

And with the sunburnt sweat
of his rippling back,
and with each heft and swing,

he showed me how to cut
a home from a red hillside.
So with a shaping word
I have tried to hew
a human place from high sun
and the hunger within
the world's rich clay.

Once I Was a Starling

Once I was a starling, hungry
hopping the dry grass full
of conversation and darkness
on the hard morning after.

Once I had the flight of clouds
engrammed into my yellow
seeing, rich in knowledge
of seeds and insects but I

a lover of trash and willing
to drag from what is abandoned
something of value to fill
the constant hunger.

Once I was able to flock
and roll as one with hidden
insight into the right time to
turn or swirl or land in tree

or come to a drop in lawns
or cornfields, one with all
who communed in sky.
Once I knew when to life

myself into flight along with
hundreds of others, leaving
only an occasional feather
as signature for this art.

Once I was a starling, and then
the time came to leave that
wisdom behind, becoming
forgetful and human again.

A Game

Played by children—
but do they understand
the song sung in night air
as they chance with dreams?

Once I played the song
near home—the rough
lightpole—singing out,
running in to touch free.

Now younger voices, high
pitched in celebration,
run to lay giggling hands
on the night's cold lesson.

Echoes from the streetcorner,
running home, touching free.
We search through small faces.
But do we comprehend

the singing in night air
as our voices rise against time
to play now forever
in the dewlaced grass,

and childhood slips away
to hide behind a tree?
The hands stop touching;
and we are far from Infree.

Spring Near Emile Creek: Poems of Youth (1950s)

Prelude: Inspirited

In the creek and in the mountain
once believed themselves a spirit.
Each a spirit to a place, linked
to a pair of eyes and to the ears
that could hear the spirit's voice.

Count the singular moments of a life
and each will have a place and spirit.
So back to each place in body,
the spirit likely is dispersed.
But go back in mind, the spirit lives.

He might first have heard the spirit
in his father's voice, walking
the woods together, his father's
hand bringing wild carrot and onion
from the soil, and showing deer in trees.

On a hillside in Pennsylvania,
by a creek, the boy might first
have heard the voices, or not
knowing they were his voices, may
have imagined them in sleep.

Under any rock of memory,
within those certain books he read
while cracking from his prior skins,
the boy might understand in moments
that his life is just such spirits.

He might have felt his flesh riving
in the small copse of trees
by the railroad tracks behind
the junior high, where the fire circle
and the clearing told of tramps.

He might have heard his skull breaking
open, when he oared around the riverbend
to find the open sewer foaming
white froth into the bay, metal-rich
in stench from the assembly plant.

But no matter what voices he thought he
heard, or what spirit he thought
he saw in the soil, the water, the trees
it was some blood within himself
that gave the whole thing song.

In the creek and in the mountain
each a spirit to a place, linked
to his eyes and to his ears and to his voice
that could he would be the voice.
And nothing more than that.

In Pennsylvania, in McKeesport

In Pennsylvania, in McKeesport,
the boy grew up amid coal
and steel, smoke and sound.
Winter: Snow fell mingled with coaldust.
Summer: The air was acrid with fumes.
Whistles sounded each day.

Coal barges chugged the river,
herded by white tugs
which churned brown water
into beards of foam.
The tugs shrieked shrill steam,
as did bleating black trains
that coughed and sang along
the steel rails beside the river.

At the bottom of the eastern hill
where the red bricked street met
the highway, a dark steel mill
blasted the night sky red
and smoked and whistled
the day into shifts,
echoing across the valley.

The soil glistened with glass beads
and slivers of shining glass
from the frozen black bubbles of slag
cast from the mill along the ridges
above the river, scabs
of slag, dark against the green.
The boy wore slag needles
in his hands and knees
from clambering the slopes.

Crystal, the sliver could not
be seen within flesh

except in the right angle of sunlight.
Sometimes he had to keep
the glass hidden in his flesh
until it worked itself free
in its own time.

Even the creek and red dog
(red clay gone stone)
seemed alive with mineral meaning
in Western Pennsylvanian hills,
where shining anthracite
and dull bituminous
were words he'd learned to spell,
and black stones were how
he came to know
incarnate darkness.

His father worked the steel,
welding it in bright sparks,
flashburning his eyes.
His mother carried the coal
from the coalbin in the basement
to the rumbling furnace.

And the boy wore coaldust
in his hair and on his face and hands,
like minstrel makeup,
while he waited the deep glass
needles in his flesh
to resurface like diamonds
from the heat and power
of the wounded earth.

Images From Pennsylvania

Mother made paper airplanes
from blue lined tablet paper
and had them lying on the floor
waiting for him when he came home.

He drummed the tin pots and pans
as a midget Krupa of the kitchen.

The kitchen sink was a bathtub
since there was no bathroom.
Parents bathed in the basement
in the round metal washtub.

He wore a cowboy hat and fired
a cap pistol with Hop-a-long whoops
and Roy Rogers honesty.

The patio hummed with summer wasps
and yellowjackets coloring the air
with fear until he could stand still
no longer in the terrible buzzing.
He struck out, was stung in the ear
where the knowledge of fear was most tender.

Red clay dried in the sun
to hand-shaped irregular saucers.
Left to itself, the clay curled upwards
in the heat, red flakes upturned.

Father drop kicked the dog off
the new-painted porch, held his belt
above his head, silence-cursed him.
He loved that father, when he smiled.

The brown and white dog barked
from his hillside pen, howling
alone against the night.

The clubhouse never was finished.
Its windowframes were windowless.
Its doorframe doorless.
Wood was missing from the floor.
Incomplete, it made a more perfect place
near the green woods.

Green woods begat crab apple trees.
Crab apple trees begat crab apple fights.
Crab apple fights begat games of war
in the summer afternoon after the action movie.

Green woods, trails winding as deer hooves
remembered Indian trails deeper
to the tricking August creek
that had roared through spring flashfloods
carrying mud and flood to the valley.

Creek of crayfish and salamander,
caught by hand, captived in impromptu
terrarium of cardboard box and plastic.
Dead within two days.

Sun rising behind the hill behind the house,
setting across the river, across the valley,
behind other western hills.

A balsa wood airplane sailing
from his hand against the west
towards which we were moving,
and the burning sun
which melted morning to its bitter end.

Wolf Dreams

The boy cried "wolf" in his dreams,
falling from the bed feet first
onto the throwrug on the hardwood floor.
What was he dreaming to call out
in the darkness, and fall from sleep?
His mother and father found him there,
lying on the throwrug, trembling.

***

The grass parted, and a black snake
split the high green. With a shudder,
the boy shoved the wooden handles,
ran the mower through the parted grass.
The path cut in the green revealed
the snake, split wide to the red meat
inside, trembling its life in blood.
When it ceased, the boy carried
the broken shudder of a corpse
like a miserable trophy on a branch
of the cherry tree. He laid it down
on the red clay bared by the shed,
and he buried it there. Guilt grew
like a thorn from his fear.

***

He saw a white patch in the hedges
beside the porch and, climbing within,
he found the headless rabbit corpse,
chased down by the neighbors brown
and white dog, caught, its head eaten,
its body left like some sacrifice
behind the green leaves of the hedge.
He carried it to the red clay graveyard
beside the shed. Later, when
the late sun glinted off a precious
stone behind the same hedge, within

he discovered the pearl of a rabbit's
eyeball torn from its seeing.
He made a separate grave for blind sight.

***

As summers passed, he found
a ceremony to go with the burials,
as he carried the carcass of snake,
squirrel, rabbit, insect, and bird
to the red clay cemetery by the shed.
Alone he dug their graves in
the burnt red Pennsylvania clay.
A robin who'd sought to fly
through the illusion of clarity
made by the picture window.
More dog hunted rabbit flesh,
with heads, but broken necks
so that the ears, the eyes and nose
followed the head in limp dangling motion.
He understood silence and used it for music.
He understood death as stillness and raw meat.
He understood the soul as a pearl of an eye,
in the dust behind a hedge.
Wondering later, if he exhumed them all,
would there be any glint in eye,
or light behind the bare white bone?

***

The boy sprang up from sleep,
the bed dancing underneath him.
Far from home, visiting in Michigan
and searching with his father for
a new house, in a stranger bed,
he'd dreamed a new dark dream.
In the vision, he had returned home
to an empty dog pen behind his house,
and silence when he questioned his mother,
who washed dishes and told him to clean
his room, and not to worry about emptiness.

At last, his sister, too weak for silence
led him to the red clay cemetery by the shed
and to a small mound just melding down.
He dug with his hands in the iron red
soil which stuck under his nails
and stained his shirt and pantlegs.
There was soon a glimpse of bare white.
He pulled the skull of his own dog
from the earth, its brown and white fur
still clinging in patches to the bone.

***

He screamed–and woke to darkness
as the wolfdream six years before.
This time he did not fall from the bed.
This time he knew the edge of the mattress
as a cliff beyond which was the wolf
in the dark whiteness of his dreams,
and bones and fleshless silence singing.

Under the Spinning Sky

Held by the left hand and left foot,
the boy is hurled in a circle,
the grass whirling beneath him,
his drunken uncle the center of his spinning.

Laughing at the boy's wide face
and dizzy stare, the older man
stumbles, drops the leg and lets the boy
rotate at the wrist to a stop in tall grass.

Laughing at the boy's wide face
and dizzy attempts to rise,
the uncle cries, "He's had one too many.
The boy's skinny as a rail, and useless."

The boy knows only the drunken
voice coming in breath and fumes
from the blue and white whirling sky.
He will not cry, even as his uncle

pinches him at the knee and,
laughing, stumbles back to the park bench.
As the man sits, watching the spinning
sky, he cries, "Skinny as a rail, and useless."

And the boy laughs,
bitterly, to himself, at the uncle's
wide face and stupid stare,
as the sky slowly stops its whirling.

The Sweetness of Color

Honey bees hummed in and out
of the sweet grape vines
which grew up the trellis and overhead
like a green, blossomed tunnel.

The boy walked through,
hearing the dangerous hum
of the bees which could sting
him into illness,

looking at the sun in fragments
through the thick leaves,
feeling the heat even here
under green shade.

His sister called to him,
and Eddie's freckled face
and red hair peered from
the end of the tunnel.

There was a small mewing
he could just hear below the buzz.
At the end of the tunnel,
under dark leaves,

the golden tabby lay,
squeezing out small gooey
bits of colored fur,
one after another.

She would lick each clean,
transforming it into
a closed eyed kitten,
even while she strained

to push the next from within her.
The boy knelt as if praying.
Each kitten grew from inside
the cat. He did not move,

did not notice when the sun
moved far enough to stab
down from the end of the tunnel
and blind him.

His sister sat with her
small hands clutched together.
Eddie stood aside, proud
as a midget carnival barker.

At last the tabby seemed done,
no more impossible, tiny
duplicates of herself
in different colors.

The boy picked up one,
as golden as its mother.
He felt it suckling his thumb,
and lay it down beside her.

He walked home in silence
while beside him his sister
danced and chattered,
telling him what he had seen.

Two days later, Sunday,
three of the seven kittens
had died. The tabby did not
seem to notice.

The Tent Caterpillar Wars

In August, when the air hummed
with dizzy heat and rasping locusts,
the men gathered together, long poles
in hand, hunting tent caterpillars.
Mr Stanislaw oiled the rags wrapped
at the top of each pole. The men
waddled down the street like
tightrope walkers or knights unhorsed.
Each rag was fired, and the men
jabbed orange heat at a treelimb's
fork where the gray wispy nest
hung like a veil caught from
the wind. Blackened burning caterpillars
tumbled from the flames to the red
brick street. And then, children
ran giggling to help.
He was one of them, squashing
the green, gray and yellow caterpillars
as they curled and uncurled across
the street. If he were quick,
if he stepped real hard, he could
get the caterpillar to pop like
a small bag, spurting its yellowgreen
life out in a mucous streak on brick.
Soon the air was thick with oil smoke
and the too sweet fetid odor
of hundreds of dead caterpillars.
They dried in the summer sun
to crusty stains on the red brick.
There were always hundreds, thousands
more. The boy tried to understand
the crystal of joy he felt in this war.

Giving the World Meaning

Before the world had meaning.
        he was a small boy looking
                up at the distant hill, rising

behind his house in dark green
        to the twin utility poles at the peak.
                Somehow this hill had purpose

being there, signifying there,
        high above the Youghiogheny.
                Someday he would have to climb it.

Before he could climb the hill,
        he had to understand the woods,
                know the trails, the vines which

hung from trees–how some of them
        were entwined in the branches enough
                that he could swing from them

across streams, and how others
        deceived you into putting your
                weight under them only to let

loose dropping you to breath stopping
        thud against the forest floor
                had to know the streams themselves,

the salamanders, snakes, crawfish
        that stirred along the creeks,
                the deer, fox, squirrel and birds

who knew the hill, who understood it
  by its presence there beside the stream.
    Before he could risk the aloneness

of the hilltop, he explored the paths
  at its base beside the rushing stream.
    He knew theses paths when snow covered

the entire forest floor–knew them
  when the spring melt rushed ruts
    in the loam and clay and when

summer thunderstorms flashed trees
  into stark shadows and sent the stream
    to mad flood out into the neighborhood

below the hill–knew them in dry summer
  dust, knew them in star quiet darkness,
    knew them in his wolf dreams.

Before he could succeed, he had to fail,
  giving up, withdrawing down the slope,
    his heart beating his own smallness

in his ears, the hill looming high
  and unconquered above him, the world
    too large around him, the sky too high.

He had to walk to school daily beside,
  beneath it, the twin poles drawing
    his eyes and mocking him from high above

like ruins from a silent, extinct tribe.
  Someone had climbed it. Someone had stood
    there and comprehended meaning.

Before he could understand meaning,
       he had to begin. In the spring
              of his ninth year, he stood at the base

of the hillside beside the rock outcrop
       above the stream where the vines hung.
              He waded through the water. He clambered

up the slope, the dark loam sliding away
       under his feet, and he began to conceive
              of the hill with each step. Mysteriously,

his steps brought forth red sandstone
       like ore mined from the earth's deep darkness.
              He wore earth in black stains on his pantlegs,

under his fingernails, streaked on his cheeks.
       Before he could give the world meaning,
              he had to reach the hilltop in springtime,

dragging himself by handhold and branch,
       protruding root, and with clambering step
              over the crest of the slope, to find

himself standing level on grass at the top.
       He walked to the creosoted black wood,
              stood under the poles and looked out

across the valley of the Youghiogheny:
       The city, the green trees, the brown
              river and white tugs pushing black barges,

white froths of foam like beards at the bows,
       the green hills on the other side,
              the black slag dumps gouged out of green,

the steel mill and the tower of the coalmine,
     the rails beside the river and the highway
         beside the rails, the sky above the valley

and the clouds white at the tops and
     dark underneath from their own shadows.
         His feet were singing with the climb.

His hands burned from scrapes and cuts.
     His heart made noises in his skull.
         The world seemed large enough for his meaning.

Sledding Under the Sky

The runners vibrated through the wood
against his chest, the steel
screeched against wind bared brick,
and his eyes teared with stinging cold.

His ears sang different voices,
pulsing with his blood excitement.
The hill became a blur of brown
trees and dirty snow.

Faster. He gripped the handles
of the sled, twisting the runners
to the right as he neared the level
of the street at hillbottom.

If he turned too soon, he would slam
into a rockpile and hedges.
If he did not turn in time,
he would sail out into traffic.

If he turned at the right time, the sled
would carry him up a gentle slope
to a stop, his heart thudding, his breath
in gray puffs around his face.

The runners sang on the bare
brick again, as they caught
to make the turn. He saw
the rockpile. The sled would not obey.

He felt himself lifted from the wood,
sailing in the air, felt hedge branches
reaching up to catch him,
scratching across his face.

Then he bounced, and his breath
broke away. He sucked in only
suffocation. He rolled over.
His chest heaved desperately.

He lay on his back eyeing the sky
and breathing it steam, felt the stinging
in his cheeks from wind and from the hedges,
and slowly found his lungs again.

The dull sky swirled in a dust of snow.
The gray, featureless sky.
The winter sky which rolled up
back into itself, and waited.

"Rat!"

Someone would yell, "Rat!", and boys
would run from every house with
baseball bats and rakes to chase
down to the iron opening of sewer
at the streetcorner. The squirming
brown things ran for the hole
and the bricked darkness there.
But if Lars dropped the block
in time, or if Eddie swung the rake
handle, the rat would squirt red
and shudder on the redbrick street.
Someone would shovel the ratcorpse
onto a board and they together
would parade it through the neighborhood,
cheering. He would join them afraid
to admit he was afraid, both of the rat,
and of what they had made of it.

Momentum

The rock flew from his hand
        as if it willed flight
                out of its own silent matter.

The rock flew as if envious
        of the robin sailing sky
                into the just blossomed locust.

The rock flew effortlessly,
        impelled by something in the boy
                that sought the bird's flight

and, not being able to have it,
        sought to negate the pulse
                of life in the bird's wings.

The rock flew with a dark grace,
        its arc mimicking the bird's.
                The boy's arm was insincere

and had never thrown a ball straight
        into an open mitt or past a waiting batter,
                had never found the mark when

they gathered together to smash
        brown bottles floating in the creek.
                But this time, impelled by a fear,

or an envy, or an understanding
        of the bird's flight onto the branch
                which still vibrated its coin sized leaves

from the inertia of the flight
        transferred from sky to silent tree
                this time, the rock flew certain,

the arm was true, the motion perfect.
        There was a "thuk"–as if the rock
                had struck the branch alone.

The robin stumbled from the tree,
        dropping feathers, losing its flight,
                abandoning its grace, its pulse of life.

The robin bounced three inches
        from the red clay bared by a shovel
                beneath the silent locust tree.

The bird lay still. The tree no
        longer moved. The boy stood, stunned
                by the anger of his unthought aim,

by the power of his arm to negate
        the flight, the pulse of bird.
                There was no blood. The robin's eyes

were beady, but clear. The boy
        backed away from the black feathers.
                The rock had disappeared,

transferring its stillness, its inertia
        of silence and negation
                to deny the pulse, the life of bird.

The bird lay still, its eyes useless,
        its wings folded against its breast,
                having spent its motion to the stone.

The rock flew on with the bird's
        momentum–forever–in the boy's mind
            negating the wind, the sky, the just passed spring.

The Man Trap

It was a man trap–
dug one foot deep, one foot wide,
in the middle of the well used
path along the ridge
above the hollow,
in the woods behind his home,
in the shadows of summer day.

He troweled open the dank loam.
He watched the scurrying of pale
insects, the drawing in
of partial worm after it
had been cleaved in two,
the other half wriggling
in his shovelful of soil.

He had often gone into
the woods with his bucket
and shovel and brought out
black dirt for his father's
garden. He knew the scent
and feel and wet of woods
and its dark earth.

Now he practiced hole-digging
to catch the woodstep of a stranger.
He lay dry branches, each half
an inch thick or so, across
the open hole, then brown leaves
across the branches, then dirt
until blended with the forest floor.

He paced back twenty steps,
and walked towards the man trap
as if he were the stranger
hiking through the leafshadows.
And just before he trod into

34

the hole, he stopped.
Smiled, pleased at his work.

Two days later, after the wild
thunderstorm that blasted
the high tension wires
at the woods edge, sending
a transformer into blue fits
of spark, dimming all the lights
in the neighborhood,

he walked the path again,
noting the craters where rain,
gathered above on leaves,
had fallen to earth in large drops,
splattering the dark soil.
He walked a clutter of
downfallen green leaves.

He saw culverts dug
by sudden streams.
He had to struggle through
the gripping branches of
a fallen silver maple.
He saw the smoked trunk
cleaved in two like the worm.

And from the top of the ridge,
he saw the trap collapsed,
sticks jutting up like an inverted campfire.
Some giant step had crushed into it,
leaving no footprints in the path.
There was nothing in the trap
but hole.

Grendel

When his stone-shaped head
first poked over the edge
of the hill where the redbrick
curved downwards towards Walnut Street,
they could hear him talking
out loud to himself, and the boys
would run and hide behind
the jagger bushes beside the woods.

They couldn't understand
his guttural noises, his headnods
and shakes, his awkward gestures
as he swaggered up the hill,
waddling under the weight
of the green and white
Pittsburgh Press bag
filled with daily newspapers.

So when he passed, the older
boys would throw crab apples.
"Ow stop," he'd shout, then step
towards a glimpse of red or blonde hair
snickering among green leaves;
and the boys would scatter,
laughing in fright and anger
at his ugly forehead and thick arms.

From door to door he'd teeter,
as if his massive head were
pulling him steadily groundward,
and only these sudden steps to
right or left in staggering
lurch kept him from tumbling over.
At each house he'd pause on porch
to drop a paper, and grunt some incantation.

The adults of the neighborhood
seemed not to notice, or mocked him
as their children did when his back
was turned, swaying their own heads like
angry elephants, then laughing
in uncomfortable superiority.
They mouthed his sounds,
as if they knew the words.

From inside his home, the boy
would wait in itching fear
to hear the murmuring voice.
The boy knew there was power
in this ugly head and big hands.
And not merely the power of
size or clumsy strength–
something many men had–but other power.

For when the boy ran home
from the hillside and cowered
behind the door to hear the grunting
guttural of the newspaper man,
he carried within dark dreams of himself
as a clumsy, fat bellied, t-shirted,
large headed child man monster,
teetering with a different face.

He was the one carrying newspapers.
He was the one swaying under the eyes
of strangers. He was the one struck
by apples and laughter, able only
to grunt out mouthsounds,
and swagger a massive skull back
down the hill, to the cave by
the river from which he'd crawled.

Hole-Digging

The earth opened in shovel-fulls,
and the boy learned the layers
of Pennsylvania earth ---
dark loam, red clay, brown sand,
gray gravel, gray clay.

He had no reason for digging,
no treasure to discover, no ore to mine,
no fantasies of a child to impel him
deeper into the cool earth.
He had no reason but the hole itself,
growing wider and deeper in the field
behind his house before the woods.

The earth opened in sweet death smells,
like a grave or a turning
of last year's crops in a farm furrow.
The earth opened its rich squirming life
of seed and worm, ant and root.
The earth opened to the sky.

Soil grew in hills on any side.
A shadow filled the hole.
The boy began to lose his sight
of anything except the bright distant sky.
Only the hole: dark shadow soil under,
above bright distant sky.

Only the soil in layers within.
Only the shadow and the scent of death/life.
Only the sky closing in bright circle.
Only the hole enveloping him.

The Squirm

In Michigan aloneness, isolated
from his childhood in Pennsylvania,
and from what he would grow to be,
he began the war against the ants.
Using the claw of hammer to kill
singly, or to rake open nests,
he soon had a teeming squirm
which made him furious and quiet.
In the garage he found a can of ether
his father used to start the old Ford
on winter mornings. He sprayed
the ants, then lit them in blue fire.
Black ants boiled and curled up, crisp,
full of the darkness of dangerous dreams.
He felt a madness of anger against
the blind orderliness of the anthill.
He felt the squirm that lives inside
his flesh and skull. He picked at it,
trying to crush the blackness, burn
it clear, crush out its green juices.
But when he closed his eyes that night,
the teeming squirm invaded, driving
him over the edge of the dark bed
into the black fungus of his brain.

Signaling the Sky

He dragged the sled
by the stiff icy rope
across ice mottled
with bright white snow
where it had caught
and fused despite
the swirling wind.
The sled would glide
where the ice bared
its black mystery or
spidered an opaque white bubble,
then stick where snow
hid the dark depth,
the runners scraping
harshly and his feet crunching
over the white island.

He dragged the sled,
worn from its original red
and showing raw wood through
after years of hill downsliding.
On it he'd stuffed
one orange crate full:
one red lantern
for signaling the shore;
one pocket radio
for understanding the weather;
one pack of matches,
four sterno cans,
and three soup cans
filled with homemade
black powder, assembled
in his basement
from sulphur, saltpeter,
charcoal, and rebellion
for setting the dark January
day afire in a column

of smoke and light,
signaling the sky.

Where the channel narrowed
as a promontory stabbed
like a white arrowhead
from the shoreline south
towards the bare trees along
the bare clay and stone,
the boy placed his devices
at regular intervals
above the dark underice,
across the brown where
the sandbar showed through,
and over the white places
where the snow fused
despite the wind.
He struck a match to each,
and saw the red rising
of colored smoke,
smelled the acrid black powder,
heard the roar of flame.

The boy looked against
the concrete gray sky
and saw the black smoke
rise in elemental sacrifice.
The sky did not reply
to his careful signaling
unless more swirling
of the low gray clouds
and the fracturing of heaven
into stinging windblown snow,
like summer dust from
a plowed field,
can be construed as answering.

But beneath his feet
like a rifle shot
the ice cracked sharply

as the third can burned out.
The winter stilled lake
under his near frozen feet
answered, answered his smoke
with enigmatic voice.

Satisfied, the boy dragged
home his worn red sled
and orange crate, now signal less,
though still holding:
one red lantern out of fuel,
four sterno cans
too dim to be seen,
one pocket radio with
batteries too weak to work,
and a pack of matches
burned black at the tips.

His hands tingled numbly,
the left curled stiff
around the icy rope.
His face stung red
at the nose and cheeks.
And his heart beat steadily
in his aching cold ears
having heard the answer
in the black mystery
below the gray sky,
under the opaque white ice,
beneath his burning feet.

Tree-Burning in January

He breathed the crystal air
into his lungs, sucked in so hard
he felt the cold burning his throat.

And he smiled up at the sky.
Taking his gloves off one at a time,
he blew hot breath onto his fingers
which were buzzing from the cold.
And then he grasped the trunk
of the pine tree and began to drag
it back down the hillside
to the creekside behind the Lundeen house.

Lars stood at the top of the hill,
and rolled one Christmas tree down.
It tumbled, the miniature of a larger pine
collapsing from a lumberer's saw,
waterfalling snow and dry needles
as it fell, cheered on by Lars
in red-faced, red-haired glee.
Eddie stacked the trees in the valley
until the pile grew 15 feet high.

It was early January. Trees lay
abandoned along the snowy streetside,
some still clinging bits of silver tinsel.
One even had an ornament inside,
locked to the tinkling branch, hidden.
Each tree bled needles behind in the snow,
a green-brown trail like Gretel's
from some housefront, across the street,
and down the slide of the hill to the valley.

When they could not stack the trees higher,
when they would only roll back down
the other side, they knew it was time

for the tree-burning. Eddie lit a rolled
newspaper from the matches his father
had given him, and they each touched
their own paper torch to his. Then standing
around the tree like druids, they put
flame to the stack of trees on three sides.

The dry trees roared to an orange
blast furnace that tongued the winter sky,
and cracked and heaved the wriggling air.
He looked through the wavering heat
like a lens between him and the others
who danced like Indians, whooping.
His face grew tight from the heat.
His eyes teared, from the cold he guessed,
or from the heat. Not from the wisdom
of January. Not from any knowledge.
Not from any mourning of lost Christmas.

Just the heat and cold wavering together
in the valley until the stack of trees
collapsed at last to black ash.
One dark circle in the snow in January.

Red Clay in His Veins

In the heat shimmer of July winds,
he first found words between the blue lines
of his school tablets. Surrounded by the buzzing
wasps on the patio his father had dug
from the red clay hillside, he pressed
the graphite tip of his pencil,
black like Pennsylvania coal,
into the pliable waiting of the page.
And he was amazed when words made their
show of life. Some rhythm hungered in him.
And feeling the rhythm, he found his
blood for the first time in his morning.

He could not understand their direction,
any more than he could comprehend
the sense of wasp buzz, the constant
rhythm of the muddy Youghiogheny down
in the valley below, or the silence
of the red clay itself surrounding him.
Nonetheless, these words mixed with
the rhythm hungering within him,
mixed with images of gray-bearded
writers receiving awards and applause,
became the faith that words could
somehow substitute for flesh and breath.

When he was done and sat back panting
like his dog in the July heat, there
was finally nothing but the words.
Words he would write for ten years
more until his quickening became career.
Words he would doubt as he doubted
the red clay, the Youghiogheny water,
or the wasp buzz in every spring.
Now that the red clay is distant.
Now that spring buzzes in hard ears.

Now that the words mean too little,
after the loss of young flesh and breath.

Fireflies and Hunger along the Huron River (1960s)

Rooftop Rafting

The boy discovered the car rooftop
lying along the freshly oiled dirt road
at the bend near the elementary school.
It was red, cut cleanly above where
the windows would have been.
It was perfect for sailing,
and so he shoved it into the pond nearby.
With a crooked branch fallen from
an elm behind the farmer's field,
he poled himself back and forth
across the twenty feet of shallow pond.

As he sailed the metal raft in quiet
to the center of the pond and drifted
in the almost no wind, the boy bent over
the edge of the cartop and noticed
black squiggles in the muddy green water:
A thousand tadpoles struggling for life.
He caught them in his hands and held
their black wriggling, then released
them back into the muddy swirls of water.
Each day after school, for a summer,
he'd sail the metal rooftop on the pond.

When he arrived each day, the metal
raft was moved from where he'd beached
it the night before. But he needed
to believe that this was his to sail
alone, his voyage alone, his knowledge
of the arcane wisdom of pond navigating,
his knowing of the black wriggling life there,
alone. And so he ignored the evidence.
At the end of that summer, when tadpoles
had turned floating white, or frogged
themselves to shore, he ended his pond-sailing.

Near the end of an August when another
summer had nearly burned itself out,
he remembered the pond and the rooftop.
The daily ritual of three years ago
ached in him, demanding that he return
to the pond and raft the metal across again.
He pedaled his red three speed down
the dry dust of the dirt road to the bend
behind the elementary school. He lay the bike
in the weeds not far from the railroad tracks,
and walked down the slope to the pond.

The water was low. The mud along
the banks was cracked and graywhite,
like dead tadpoles bleached along
the shore where they had drowned in air.
The rooftop lay drydocked in mud,
its red gone rusty, its smooth curve
gone dented from hundreds of feet.
The crooked stick was missing.
Still, he shoved himself off, counting
on the momentum to sail him across
the diminished width of the pond.

Immediately, brown water spurted
through a dozen holes punched cleanly
in the metal by some other boy.
The water fountained in, slowing the raft.
It stopped near the center, sank.
Brown mud scurried over the sides
and into his shoes. The boy waded
through the sucking mud squirting
swirls of gray and brown behind him.
The clear water of the pond clouded over.
He barefoot rode his bicycle back home.

Near the end of yet another summer,
when high school had begun, the boy walked
the long way home down the bend in the road
behind the elementary school.

The pond had dried to cracked clay
in the drought. The rooftop was gone,
taken by someone somewhere.
And he remembered the tadpoles left behind
that had turned to frogs in the river
or gone graywhite in the still dust
where the sun had transformed them.

Just the Night

The boy sat with two friends
on the sand where the dark lake
echoed waves back and forth
to splash against each shore.
He could hear the water across
the lake when it beached against
the bay near the trees where
Denton road made a sharp bend.
And then, after a long pause,
the water would again lap
the sand beside his feet.

An older friend sat on the other
side of flames, smiling as firelight
licked his face with red tongues
and dark shadows.
There were four log fires–one
at his feet, one in each eye,
and one floating in the water beside them.

"On Denton Road at night,
the older boy said, "there's this
light, red, and it moves by itself
between the trees in the summer.
No one knows what it is.
Some say its a rotting stump.
Some say its light bent from
a star or from a house far off.
But I know it's not either.

"If you go in there, at night,
in the summer, like this night,
you can't even catch it.
There it is, a red dot, moving
in and out of the trees. If you
try to get near, it moves away.

52

If you move away it comes out
of the woods and waits at the bend
in the road. If you stay still,
it stays still, as if watching.

"One spring, about 75 years ago,
a wagon overturned there,
and its lantern fell and somehow
didn't break but kept burning.
The driver was crushed underneath.
He lay there for hours, trying
to reach the red lantern and signal
someone across the lake. He died.
They found him with his fingers
just inches from the handle.

"Some say, at night, in the summer,
he's still reaching for the lantern
trying to signal help for his soul.
Some say he's got ahold of it
and carries it with him, back and forth,
trying to warn others away from
the sharp bend in the gravel road there.

"But I know he's trying to draw
you into the woods. I say he tries
to siren others into death at the turn
of the road. They may drive cars now.
You might walk, or pedal your bike.
But if you get near the woods
at night, in the summer, like tonight,
the red light will hypnotize you.
Turn too quick at the bend,
come too close to the woods,
and he's got you!" And the older
boy laughed, the red firelight flickering
on his wet and shining teeth.

The boys laughed too, and braved
themselves up, mocking each other
for being afraid, then traded stories
of Dracula in the trees, and monsters
creeping up from the dark water beside them.
They talked until the gooseflesh thrill
left them for drowsiness and boredom.
Then the older boy quenched the fire
to red coals glowing in the sand.

Later that night, in the canvas
tent smelling of old rainstorms
and mildew, the boy is awakened.
He sits up in his bedding, the sand
sifting underneath him and kicking
up onto the plaid blanket on top.
A red light beats on the tent wall
around him, and he sucks the dark
night air into his mouth with a gulp.

He wants to wake the two boys beside
him, but fears their mocking laughter.
So he parts the tent flap himself
and stares across the silent lake.
Stars lie on the water, wavering
with the waves that still echo
bank to bank. An elongated moon
settles into the trees above the bay.

And a red light flashes steadily
where the police have parked beneath
the moon. The boy giggles nervously.
Just a false alarm. Just the ghost
stories and the night and sleep.
He ducks his head back inside
the tent and huddles under the bedding.
He watches the red light throbbing,
and tries to tease himself into grinning
at the night. Water beats against
the sand beside the tent.

And the police stand on the opposite
shore where a car has missed the turn
at Denton Road, and plunged
into the lake and the dark water.

Shouting "Run" into the Brain

In early October, when only
those trees that always
leaved first and lost first
were changing   like the silver
maple by the highway
he went behind the house
to burn trash in the incinerator,
and found his dog running madly
while lying on its side.

It was the only dog of his
thirteen years. Now it ran,
its eyes sealed, its muscles
answering the madness as in
a dream. The boy called out
the dog's name, trying to wake
it from its dream running.
The signals within the dog still
shouted "run" and muscles still obeyed.

His father, whose stone face
the boy could never read except
in anger, told him, "Get away!"
and gently gathered the dog
in his arms. The tanned muscles
of his father's jaw tightened,
his eyes grew distant as he placed
the running mad dog in black
Country Sedan, and closed the tailgate.

"Get away," his father said again.
The boy ran to the highway,
climbed the yellowing silver
maple there till he got to
the first wide fork, then sat,
his arms embracing the black

rough bark, as if it were his father.
He sat there in the crotch
of tree, his own legs trembling.

He kept his back to the dirt road
down which he heard the black car
rippling its tires across gravel.
In his sealed eyes the boy saw
his dog still running, its toenails
scratching against the red paint
of the car interior as his father
drove death's dark signals to a distance.
The boy sat still till he heard silence.

He opened his eyes to the leaves
around him, some still green,
some already curled in brown,
most brilliantly yellow in October.
The air was warm enough he
didn't need his jacket. There
was no wind. He felt the madness
of his legs which trembled,
shouting "run" into his brain.

Fireflies

Along the tracks south of town
the boy lined gravel stones
one by one, six inches apart,
standing on the shining steel.

When he had placed twenty,
he stood in the center of
the westbound track, on a tie,
and he looked east.

There was a kind of minor sun
wavering there. A train
headlight hesitated in hot
summer air. The boy waited,

bouncing on his toes, looking
towards the light then studying
the twenty stones.
The real sun cast long shadows.

The ground began to vibrate.
The diesel engine neared.
Its light brightened, and
the diesel wailed its warning

crossing Huron River Drive,
just a mile away. The boy
ran from the rail to the tall
weeds and cattails bedside.

The engine grew huge, its wheels
whirling over the shining steel rails,
hauling a mile of red, orange, brown
and black rail cars.

The horn sounded for Martinsville Road,
the ground rumbling now beneath him.
The real sun sank in red
to the west where the train was destined.

As sudden as death the engine
was above him, black and roaring,
a small man in a red cap sitting
with right arm out the open window.

And as it passed, its song howled,
hesitated, then dropped in pitch,
its shining steel wheels
where they met the shining steel rails

crushed the twenty gravel stones
in quick succession, sending
bright flinted sparks into the air
and dry grass along the tracks.

The sparks did not catch.
The train did not derail,
but clicked on as each wheel of boxcar,
car carrier, reefer met the joint in steel.

He had wanted to see the power
of the sun in those steel wheels
meeting the twenty stones
across the steel rails.

He had wanted to make the sun
spark like fireflies in the night.
And he had waited to see if the power
would overturn the black, pounding diesel.

After the train had passed and
its rumble diminished to distant
humming in the rails and ties,
the boy stepped from the tall grass.

He stood again on the shining rail.
Not even dust where the stones had been.
The train had become one wavering red spot.
In the air around him fireflies sparked.

Just Stars, Dew and Darkness

He lay in the grass,
sensing the fall of dew
from the black night
as it soaked his clothes
and dampened his skin.
But his eyes focused
again and again
on the stars.

His spine knew the hard
outline of ridges
of earth beneath him
under the thick bladed grass
which had folded down
into a shape that
was his.

But even as he lay,
sighting from
star to star, his mind
storied within him.
Instead of lying alone,
he lies with a girl,
maybe Mary Jane
who calls him ugly
and showed him her panties.
Maybe here, he wasn't ugly,
underneath these stars.

They two would try to feel
the heat of ancient light
falling down against them.
as they lay in a wetfield
in the country south
of Carleton, after 1 am,
quiet like lovers.

He was conscious of
something meant by the stars
burning out of dew
in the quiet darkness.
He heard the thump
of blood in his ears
and in his throat,
tried to concentrate
on the August sky
where a fall of meteors,
the Pleiades, was expected.

But he kept sensing this girl
beside him, kept knowing
her heat, her breathing.
He edged his left hand slowly
outward until it would touch
her bare arm near the shoulder.
Suddenly she drew back,
disappearing from the grass,
the dew, the darkness.
His hand curled up clutching
the wet grass like her hair.

A sudden star streaked across the sky–

Just a burning rock descending
too close to the world,
and flaming itself out
in orange and silent
disintegration.

The Hungry Circle

He studied a circle of light
in the black cylinder of the microscope,
and viewed the leg of a fly
hairy and backwards-jointed,
sprouting with angry blackness
from the bright white circle behind.

He watched the amoeba suck and throb
across its bit of pond water,
transparent in its guts
to his hungry naked vision.

He grew sugar and salt crystals
on strings in glasses of water,
then peered through their
rainbow shadows on the slides.

Through the tunnel of the lens,
he watched for "Sea Nymphs" to hatch
as the advertisement had promised,
"amazing" to him and his friends.
But though he followed the instructions,
brewing a saltwater ocean for them
in jar, nothing lived.

He scraped his own skin from his arm
and studied his cells. He pricked
his own blood to feed the pelican
young of his own imagination.
But he could not puzzle out
why he should be here, living,
watching, waiting in a circle of light.

A cat hair of a million whiskers
hid its knowledge of night and tight places.
The dust from a dozen formaldehyded
moths and butterflies kept real sight from him.

No glass of water was truly incorrupt.
No sample of soil didn't teem
with wriggling, hungry eating.
No object didn't have a hidden life,
wonderful, ugly, and incomprehensible
despite the black hollow of crystal light.

He began to see the world as if
his own eye were the round eyepiece
of the microscope, as if he were like
Ray Milland in "The Man with X-Ray Eyes."

The more he looked, the more he knew
that for the ten years he had lived,
though he had been a running, breathing,
sucking life, moving like an amoeba
across some larger circle of pond water,
he had not been aware, he had not seen.

The more he looked, the more he fell
into the vision tunneling though the cylinder,
into that two-dimensioned world
held within the circle's bounds.

The more he felt himself drawing out,
into separation, away from the world,
the more he wrote double-spaced stories
in his basement in the coal cellar
he'd rebuilt into his own monk cell.

Seeing the way made him something.
As soon as he knew his own self
as something he could study in
a circle of light, he felt the planet
draw away from him beneath his feet.

As if a mother woke one day
and found a stranger wearing
her son's face, and sent him
away from herself, into an exile
where the knowing lived.

The Thousandth Face

Three times a week for a year
and a half, he walked the tracks
to the secret copse between
plowed fields. Yes, the farmer
knew the trees he plowed around.
And the railroad engineer
saw them as he roared by,
dragging a hundred railcars.
The secret was not the copse itself.
The secret was not that
the boy went there,
three times a week, alone.

And he kept to himself the thousand names
his classmates called him daily.
What was secret was that
when he entered the copse he
became a coureur, an explorer,
an Indian, a wild animal–
anything but the twelve year self
he hated–for its scrawniness,
its clumsiness, its glasses
and big nose, its gangly
ugliness of indeterminate
state, and its aloneness.

Here, his secret of aloneness
was pure, and became the copse
of trees, which while he was within
extended itself to infinities.
He had a thousand choices.
Each choice led out of the copse
by a different path to a different
self. He had a thousand futures.
He had a thousand other faces.
Here his isolation became a cause

66

to crusade against the schoolday.
Here his aloneness was heroic.

He would sit on the fallen oak
and study the green ceiling
and the pattern of sun and shade
on the dark loam floor.
He would touch the ashes
of a fire some drifter had set,
searching the abandoned campsite
like a tracker hunting an outlaw.
Near dusk, he'd follow one of the paths
out of the copse, searching
for the thousandth face, the thousandth
future–the one that would become him.

When he left the copse each day,
three times a week for a year
and a half, he took any path
that brought him back to the tracks
in time for the sun to lay down
against the shining rails where
they converged at the red horizon.
It was done quietly. He would walk
the glowing tracks home till
they quenched in darkness.
He had a thousand faces with him,
burning in deep red within.

Memorial

He watched the orange rocket
leap at the young blue sky
in a curved line of white smoke
and saw in it the arc of his future
like a blinding sun against
a cloud. The old super-eight
millimeter movie now
transferred to fidgety tape
shows a silent rocket jumping
from the ground in half speed.
But in his ears he still hears
the whoosh of a door opening
briefly before closing his sight.

Chasing Loons

He clung to the slick bow
of the speeding Sea Ray,
the 110 horse Mercury roaring
behind his wind-driven ears.
The dancing bow thumped his chest
against the beige fiberglass
on each fall into wave trough.
Cold spray splintered against his face.

The loon flew just out of reach
of his grasping right hand.
It's clumsy flying reminded him
of the joy and humiliation he felt
when he wanted Anne.
He laughed at the loon
as he had been laughed at.
He strained to reach the loon
as the motorboat seemed ready
to drive him into its flight.

Suddenly, the loon staggered right,
faltered, then fell from the wind
into the green April water.
Ed throttled back,
and the prop cavitated,
gurgling and popping in white bubbles.
They both looked at the water
where the loon had fallen.
It was stained with ripples.
But there was nothing else.
No feathers. Just circles of absence.

He thought the bird must have
broken its heart in its shame and fear.
He thought the bird must have
died, falling from the wind.

They idled the boat in circles,
looking for the loon corpse.
Ed finally turned the motor off
and let the boat drift with
the early dank wind
which stung the face and remembered
quietly the sound the engine had made.

Suddenly, a hundred feet away,
downstream, towards the dam
the loon cry, mourning,
no, the loon laugh, haunting.
As it had been laughed before.
As it would always be laughed.
The same loon fallen from the wind.
Immortal. Shameless. Sudden.
The same laugh in the morning.

Sun and Brown Water

The youth swam in the brown river,
bumping his feet against slow carp
that gape mouthed near the surface
in the hot sun and warm water.

He drifted across the currents,
feeling the cool upsurge of one,
and the swift warmth of another.
The river was quiet just now.

The water skiers and roaring boats
were beyond the point in the curve
of the river. And this was a weekday.
He floated in the calm of a cove.

The youth allowed the water its will
and lay back, the sun blinding him
in gold and heat across his chest.
Without his glasses, he could still

see the sky for what it was.
A quick breeze danced over him–
but it was too warm to chill him.
He knew he was at the end of summer–

the emptiness of sky above
filled him with its knowledge.
He dove into the muck below,
blindly touching the river bottom.

He could stay there and never surface.
Or he could burn his flesh in sun.
Whatever way the water willed,
he'd drift the right way, seeing.

Storm Sunset

Across the flat water and low islands
of St. Clair, the squall line rolled
black, lightning testing the water.
Thunder road the waves to him, standing
before the cottage on the island.

The canoe bounced against the dock
where he had tied it with yellow cord.
The wind flagged his pant legs, lashed
his eyes with his own hair, made ocean
roar in the hollows of his ears.

In three months he'd ride to Fort Wayne,
show the scar on his thumb, and leave
his black fingerprints on white paper.
In three months he would be waiting
out the dark war over the horizon.

"Come on inside," Ed shouted to him.
But drawn to the sound like cannon
over the western horizon, his nostrils
wide to the scent of distant rain,
he heard only the darkness shouting.

The others retreated to the shuttered
porch, where they sat on the resonating
floor nervously playing euchre
and laughing a bit too loudly.
He stood outside in sun and shadow.

He moved only with the wind, watching
the stormline, like a cavalry charge
of black horses and black riders,
flashing sabers, shouting like wind,
and riding the thunder of gunfire.

Driftwood Memories or Waiting for Fire - 1972

Waiting for Fire

At the apex of roads
in the middle of prairie, asleep
like a waiting prairie fire,
he has abandoned the carstreams
for this dried, baked clay,
this scrub-brush, these sandfleas.

For two nights, he had not slept,
trying to outwit his eyelids
until his eyes were hot
and clumsy, as dry as Wyoming.
The road at night was bloody
with taillights. Mesas and
crag-faced mountains shadowed
the thin-starred darkness
as he found rides with strangers
in their dark cars.

At dawn, this day, he'd been emptied
onto this prairie, unrolling
from a dusty brown Falcon
into a sleeping bag thrown
over a nearflat place to sleep.
When he wakes, he wakens to
a white sun. Every stone,
every crack, every scar
in the dry clay mapped
into his dull flesh.

Two swigs of tepid tinny water
from the canvas covered canteen,
and he rises to the road again
to hitch still further west,
away from the concrete,
the dry heat, away from
the empty prairie within.

He Tries to Hear the Mountains

He had wanted to hear the mountains.
Instead there was distant silence,
angles of light, color, and the power
of a colder wind blowing down, carrying
the scent of pine and touch of snow.

He had wanted to hear the mountains.
He heard just his own beating, breathing,
the scruff of his bootsoles on gravel,
and the voices behind his denying.

He shifted the pack, and rose to the foothills.
The wind and the voices fought for his
shadow which cast itself back eastward
from the clear white outline of distant
light and shadow and the power.

The colder wind blew down across his dust.

Walking Towards the Mountains

Middle day heat shimmered
above the asphalt and black ash.
White pine wriggled in the haze.
His sweat ran into his eyes
as he fought the backpack, fought
the straps, fought the dry ground
which, kicked up into his face,
drew black rivers from his cheeks.

Every quarter mile brought him
down against a tree, against
its rough peeling bark, and against
the sharp brown grass below.
The heat, the road, the furious
faces of passing cardrivers
seemed to slow his steps,
touching him against tree
after tree along the roadside.

His watch still wore another
time, three hours fast,
when he put it off in a pocket.
Stopped at the daylast tree,
his eyes followed the sun
down in true time.

And though he camped by a lake
and the night cooled, he slept
in the fire of that angry first
day, alone, near flames from
dried broken fallwood, until
night gathered him in, and
grew red in conflagration.

Waiting in Shadows

Quick eyes couldn't see the changes
as the snow remained, cold wind persisted;
but spring greened in bare places,
and the fishing hole first day opened,
filling with Oregonians who cast
lines out and pulled back trout.

He'd been given a ride with a fishing
family in the back of their pickup
over a fireroad near Three Sisters.
He'd been given a map by the driver,
and a way bypassing snow
to the trails in the foothills above.

But his quickeyes couldn't find
the trails under ten feet of snow
burned hard by early July heat.
So he waited in cool green shadows,
watched poles flash, silk leap
in slow arcs to plunk lures down
in pools of ice runoff.

He heard the mad plashing fight
of fish, couldn't hear rightness
in their deaths, could feel only
the cold snow wind blown off
the mountains and down his bare neck.

He didn't fish, left the shadow and
snow-encircled pool, left the whiz
of reels, the raucous laughs and
popping Coors, and walked again
in high sun, going higher, quickly.

Morning Refuses Him

Hooves woke him from red dreams
of a twenty-year old fire
beside the shallow lake.

A brown buck pawed old ash
in the doe-circle, snorting
grey clouds of morning.

He unzipped from his cocoon
and offered himself. The buck
arched away, thumping in dusty echoes.

The buck answered an instinct.
But he stayed himself, stayed
separate, and knew that was no way.

A Day of Falls

From the birthing sun, fire
blazed his eyes, coloring
the morning rage red. He shielded
his sight with his hand, but
that first fire broke, poured
down his arms like sweat
into the stream below, reddening
the cascade of water. From
fifty feet above, pink mist
tumbled in a fall to white
froth and green water. The fire
drew some poison, bleeding
him clean. With sunflame at
his back, he faced the mountains.

Green conifer grew moist here
in the valley. Moss clutched
to stone for drink and food.
Descending as the water, he
found his drysteps and the hot
July morning cooled by the breath
of the valley under falls.
The Tumulo, wild and hungry
like a Klamath, misted
and cooled him from memory.

He lost some chance there.
And fast the sun slammed down
in heat and fire against the Rockies.
The falls curled over in surprise
and colored with broken rainbows.
For a day the mist cooled
his face. But he wiped the water
away, like sweat, and worked
at walking towards some sleep.

Bridge of Snow

Quietly, the river swept beneath
him as he stood on snow.
He didn't know its presence
until, downhill, it disgorged
from a cavern of blue ice.

He had balanced above the wild
springmelt, and hadn't plunged
through to its dark water.
He had balanced fifteen feet
above where the ground paused,
waiting this weight of winter.

Quietly, he climbed, subdued
by the hidden risk, and rush.
He camped in a rot-warmed circle
swept clean in the center of snow.
He lay awake in dark silence,
no wind, no crickets, no leaves
to sound the air.

Turning his face to the clear
black, star-crystaled night,
he knew there was no one.

Not a Rib

Something broke inside on the slide
down the snowbank; lost balance
and the topweighted backpack dragged
him over, crashing down against a tree.
Something cracked — not a rib, not
a bone or an organ at all. Something.

He lay in the wind-carved hole
around the tree, a circle embanked
in snow. He felt himself over
carefully for injury, and found none.
The tree itself helped him stand,
then rise from the windhole, balancing
himself with the touch of green branches.

Standing on the topedge, looking down,
he saw the dim outline of his shadow
broken around the treetrunk below.
Something broke inside. Not a rib.

Confronting the Edge

Thrashing through branches,
blood thundering in his ears,
he strode like a citystreet
walker, not a one of woods.
The pack swayed on his back,
stuck against pinebranches
and tore needles in a shower.
He ran from his own clouded step.
Unminded, he thought too much.

Flash of light and fifty feet
of cliff dropped bare in front
of him. Stop. The heart flies on,
pounding away. The eyes fall
over the edge and dash against
the rockfall below. The body
quavers between the momentum
of the pace and the stillness
at the cliff. So close to the edge.

He sits, spreads map across
his lap. He looks from colored
lines to green fir and brown
rock. The map is not this place.
Is it the wrong map? Or is Map
all wrong? South lay dead over
the cliff. The sun arced there
above the ridge of pine. Somewhere
hidden, the road to Bend Oregon.

He waited till the march of his
heart stopped, then rose, thumbs
shoved up under straps, shifting
the pack upright. East, downhill,
in a different motion, with his
life at the cliffedge. And the map?

It lay above him at the place
of confrontation,
on the rock, at the cliff, unused.

Sleeping Near the Edge

Beside the long, curved trail,
at night, near sleep,
he lies under the now moonless sky
trying to discover shapes in stars.
He breathes the day's walking
with the sweet evergreen.
Both the cold dew and the dark
smoke cling to him. The night's
silence dissolves older scents.
A bird rustles leaves.

Near the edge, almost in tune
with larger voices and the dome
of black sky, he can almost
cease his brain's ceaseless
insect buzzing. Almost.
Tonight he sleeps nearer
that huge silence. He fears
it less than the long
curved trail back home.

Confronting the Other

He moved in dawnlight,
following the redfox trailblazer
who leapt from behind a white pine,
froze against a snowbank,
then scurried over undulations
of blue drift and shadow.

Something from the light
of snow and sun struck his
still night eyes. The weight
of his pack, like the weight
of his body, slipped from him
into a more than human motion.

Why presume that the snow
drifted, the sun glinted
just at the right angle,
the trees waited, and the fox
halted all just for him?
There was no one else.

Flash of fox in snow,
bounding the drifts in silence.
Rich aromas of spring fir.
His feet fall down the hillside.
His thoughts wait behind in
shadows of fox memory.

Bend, Oregon: The Fourth of July

Tall pines, bed needles beneath,
ash below rock precipice:

He has come to an end of
denials, and flows with the cold
stream of melting ice.
He cuts deep with the rivulets.
He molds crevices in mud.
He tears with the falling water
and leaps rapids of rock and time
diving for the valley.

Surrounded there by sorties
of mosquitoes, water wrigglings
of snakes, he drifts through swamps
in lazy near stagnation
to the waterfall, and midair dances.

He becomes mist.
He powers the small generators.
He runs to the city
and becomes the river,
suspends the swimming children
and the sailboats highing to the wind;
and he reflects fireworks by night.

He sleeps there one night
beneath a park bench, unpoor hobo,
awaiting the change
to peacefulness and deep moving.

Before Such Eager Firelight

He stalked into the campground,
wearing a beard and a pony-tail,
looking some wildman or trailblazer---
scrawny, but burned hard by the sun.
The showers were free if you paid
your three dollars, and took your place
on the campsite as if you were
a Winnebago. And so, for a night,
he would sleep surrounded by campfires.
He threw his pack to the ground.

Across the dirt roadway, a man signaled.
"Come over and have some dinner with us."
He walked the crunching gravel in his
bare feet, and sat near the short man
and his fatter wife. A young girl just
taking woman's shape came from the camper.
"She's our niece. She's been in trouble.
Her mother's divorced and can't handle her.
She keeps running away. So we took her
for a vacation here in southern Oregon."

As the light faded to red campfire,
he told them of his journey, not its
real purpose, which he didn't know,
but of its shape in car-rides, hot
walking, and sweat in cold mountains.
He paid the wage of all way-farers
who eat at another's fire: He told his story.
The young girl watched him with
eager firelight in her eyes. He was
amazed at the power in his telling.

When morning came, the short man
offered to drive him to the highway,
sending him in graylight back to

his road way and day walking.
"You needn't thank me for the lift.
It's not just a favor to you.
Jenny told us last night, when
we had our regular fight with her,
that she was going to run away with you.
Did she tell you she was planning that?"

He said he'd told her nothing but his story
while they were alone beside the campfire.
But he remembered the eager firelight
in her eyes. And he wondered what
it would be like to know her eyes
and her body in the silent firelight
above the treeline in the mountains.
He left the car like a criminal,
and signaled the next driver to take
him anywhere away from his crime.

Blocked by a Mountain Stream

When a swollen angry stream
crossed his path and stopped him,
he stood, some dumb spirit,
some wound of eyes and mouth and ears
spilling itself into the dark sound
of water. He had walked in dream
of self for days over snowmelt
rivers hiding their violent rumbling
beneath blue ice, while July burned
his flesh,. He had forded crystal
springlakes that were as cold
as his remembering. But when he
came to this sluice of white water
roaring like old wars over rocks,
he knew it would consume his walking.

And then it seemed like sleep:
the walking, the remembering, his homeplace.
He stood for hours, uncomprehending,
silent, then woke to a black painting.
Starlight silhouetted treeshapes
around him. Night held no more demons;
just cold stars, this black veil,
white snow on the hillside, pinesmell,
thin rattlings of leaves by nightbeasts,
breathings in the wind. And the pulse,
the rush of water, the movement
of identities to course and sound.
Near sleep now in his sleeping bag,
he would cross the dark water downstream
when it slowed its wet creation.

Gifts of Sanctuary

First case:

Along Highway One in California,
cold, wet, sick, he left the road
to find a well-worn arcing path
to a shelter long prepared:
a hole in a mossy redwood,
home for a green lizard
and a human for one night.

Too weak to make an evening fire,
too tired to eat the hard tack
in his knapsack, he saw a sudden ghost
emerge sodden from the mist.
Lean and tall like the Redwoods,
a hitching sailor freed from the Navy
asked to join him in the hutch of tree.

Seeing how sick he was, the sailor
made a fire, cooked him food,
offered him a menthol in hopes
it would clear his lungs, and told
him stories of the sea so he
could drift into a safer darkness,
and so be ready for the morning road.

Anemic smoke of the wet fire rose
as fog, congealed in pine needles
and plopped down to the forest floor,
as rhythm to his sleep. The tree
closed around them, drew them
into itself, like water, made them flow
inside. He breathed himself into mist.

Second Case:

Alone again, he hitchhiked hot
north through Oregon to Washington
where thick brown thunderstorms
introduced him to Rainier. He could
see through the mist as lightning
fingered the mountain, and two
rainbows arced above the pass

Rainier rained daily, the driver
told him, as he offered him a lift
on US 12, and laughed at him for
arriving tentless to a rainforest.
From his trunk the driver offered him
a box of Nilla wafers and a plastic
tube tent to string between two trees.

Near Deer Creek, he camped,
the valley echoing with thunder,
the water channeling in the ruts
he'd carved around the blue canopy.
He slept in exhausted peace
within the gift, alone, dreaming
the rain drops plopping near his head.

As High as He Could Go

He plodded the hairpinned road
in a gray mist of morning,
an initiate, waiting.

At a certain elevation,
the clouds of the lower land
dissipated. He stood above them.

Sun slashed through open blue,
sluicing off the sheer white blinding
of the glacier. He blinked.

Touching against the cold unreason,
the sharp irregular angles,
the bluewhite that was Rainier,

he almost saw himself clear.
He did not plod the hairpins down,
but ran through the green between.

Preparing Supper the Last Time

As the sun sets the water
red across a still lake,

as the meal steams in the blackened pot,
fire snapping at the cooling air
and lifting echoes of red sparks
in the smoke that swirls uphill
to a rockpeak overhanging the lake,

as the yesterdays that buzzed
around an aging face
like mosquitoes, burn off and
drift away with the smoke
in essential sacrifice,

as dusk ripples with
the wingthrusts of a crane
flapping up from reeds,
its image downshrinking in rose water,

as memories lie quiet now
and the present bloods louder
like an earpulse after running,

he quietly becomes the silence,
fills with new breath,
as if the wind had changed,
as if supper tasted fresh,
as if the sun had become
red water cupped in his hands
as an offering to dry lips.

A green afterimage lingers
in his eyes past nightfall,
a ghost sun, reflected moon
in mirrored water, following

94

the light down into its own image,
but still.

If the Moon Hadn't Come in Time

He fought against his own sleep,
turning fitfully in cold leaves,
restless on damp earth near
the swamp. Broken limbs cracked,
clutched his ripped clothing;
twigs stuck to him like quills.
He rolled himself in the dregs
of a season of felled trees.

False colors trembled his eyelids.
Images dreamed in him:
Cliffs lurching from behind pine,
dropping fathoms to rockfall;
rushes of winds and white creeks;
cold sun blinding him from
dunes of snow beside dunes of sand,
with mounds of green weed between.

While he tumbled in bright sleep,
the dark swamp began to swallow him.
Humming mosquito clouds drank him,
leaves and soil covered him,
and water snakes whirled in him,
challenging the union to absorb
him without being him.

Before the two met, place and man,
world and word becoming one
meaning, a sparkling off a wet f
ern scraped against his eyes with
the pale flicker of double-glanced
light. He awoke to wide stare.
The moon had broken through trees.
The shadow had withdrawn its chance.

Motion and Movement

The day's motion still ticked
in his veins, as he lay in sand,
watching the wind manifest itself
in the slow movement of tall reeds.
Stars wove themselves into
the night sky. But none of it
connected. There was no entry
for him through the growth
and loss around him. At last,
he fell for the communion
of a poor dream.

In the gray dawn of reed and
weed, moving in nightborn wind,
a hummingbird, whirring soft
blurwings, sucked flowers, its
small body motionless in movement.
Just out of hand's reach, the brown
center of energy darted away,
turning from his human quickening
to overcast sky. Too near
the losing self, he fell
for another day.

Bridge of Steel

Howls from the bridge
slice through the hills,
echoing in the barren riverbed,
waterless and pebbled.

The sleeper bends in dreams
to the river, now dried
into a trickle between smooth stones
His fire, cupped by a boulder,
lifts red embers to the sky,
where redcracks of sparks
imitate the stars.

Still howls from the bridge
echo at memories.

He doesn't hear screams
from the highway downstream
on the arching bridge
he crossed at sunset.
He hears instead the absent
water of the empty bed
remotioned by dreams to a flow.

The current in night carries
him, as the river cannot,
as the howls cannot prevent,
to morning.

There, he builds a breakfast
from the red coals of yesterday.

Facing Backwards

High in a hotel room in Tacoma,
he has come back to city rhythms.
The ocean is too far from him.
The memory of the confrontation
 is too near to be understood.

He strips, takes a shower, washes
the odor of smoke and pine needles
and his own walking sweat
from his body. And he washes his
clothes clean in the shower stall.

Sitting on the bed, naked, his
clothes hanging like shadows
from the curtain rod, he suddenly
feels Rainier's cold image on a calendar.
There were the days of his journey:

Numbered clear. Black on white.
He rises from the creaking bed and
walks to the east window. Sudden,
naked, Rainier rises above the flat
green. It was no dream.

The bluewhite clearness in bright
outline against the quick blue sky.
The shadows across the flat green.
The squat flat clouds moving westward
towards him in the dark hotel.

Sleeping with Stone

He woke suddenly from twisted sleep
on the hard flat stone on the hill
in the park above Spokane. He woke
to voices from yellow windows
in houses around the park.

His back had stiffened to the stone.
His eyes found soft yellow light
foreign. He lay back against rock
and watched the slow whirl of cold stars.

It would take a hundred days
to stop sleeping with the rock.
It would take a hundred days
to stop watching with the stars.

And when a hundred months have passed,
the hardness of the rock will save him,
the clarity of stars return him home.

Against the Concrete

After bright snow bridges
and rushing caverns of water,
he is found now beneath concrete
in the rush of city traffic, before
the opening of the cave of overpass.

He sits against the abutment.
He peels an orange and feels the wind
of passing cars. He is a dark presence
without a soul of his own,
and without the anger to invent one.

The sea rhythms his pulse now.
The mountain casts itself against
the inside of his eyes, a bright
shadow. Then a salesman stops his
LTD, and carries him back eastward.

The Last Terminal

The bus chugged into the Chicago Terminal
spilling out diesel fumes, hissing, stopped.

Lost was the backpack crated away
somewhere in the interchange of buses.

Lost was the last fifty dollars.
This was an end, not a junction.

The buses coughed, eyes watered.
Nonhuman voices loudspeakered

destinations no one understood.
A girl blankly told him how

she'd been raped by some truckdriver.
An English tourist wondered why the roads

couldn't stop, the country couldn't stop,
why it went on in summer and mad traffic.

He slept half-sleeps in a black plastic
whosebody chair steeled to other chairs.

He dreamed of snow and trees
while the voices droned around him

in terminal echoes, and his bus
left him behind. There would be others,

whining with turbines, ready to take
him home to meet his lost backpack,

emptied now like life left behind in mountains
with the sunfading snowprints of journey.

Alien Shape

Within the pile of seapiled drift-trees,
in the kingdom of sandfleas
and driftwood termites,
he lay as stranger, flowing inward
with the rush and lapse of ocean waves
pilfering the sandshore.

Fog clouded the issuing,
then swirled inland, deeper,
containing the world in a seacircle
paled by moonsight.

There as the sand molded itself
in the human shape of the sleeper,
as the coals of a suppered fire
heated the sand beneath his body,
the stranger died, flowing inward.
Journeying in the open dreamworld
of sandsea and unrepressed energy,
he is found.

Coda: The Journey

There suddenly surged in him as
the ground fell away

a river that designed his eyes to
its cold flowing.

The water lived in his flesh and
in his open eyes.

He saw the life of the barest electron,
the darkest rock,

and the whole flood that was
the universe

spinning out of his control.
If only he could see

deep enough, small enough, far enough,
the will would end.

He would not drown but turn river,
himself just liquid.

His face began to swim away from
its identity.

His senses closed together in
one distinct taste,

that of a salt sea on a cold day.
He tried to pull

himself away from it, from the waves
and their crashing,

but the sudden mist sprayed up across
his bearded face,

masking the clear white vision
of the blue mountain.

He slept In blackness. He
dreamed of nothing.

When he awoke, drained, dried,
sunbleached on

a brownblack, creviced rock jutting
out into a tided and

stilled ocean, he remembered the silence
as a dream

where the journey was the dreamer,
and he its image.

Poems from Short-Grass Prairie to Salt Shore

Tenses

He sailed an ocean, not a map,
an ocean of grass and grain
and concrete trails thru it all,
an ocean of fir needles and loam,
an ocean of ferns and fog drippings.
For yeardays all turnings sped
in a grave course of gray clouds.
And now there were motions of gold.

Open lands, open furrows,
lips up for the wind,
between the hills and arteries of rivers.
One night in downtown linen,
one night in the arms of driftwood treetrunks.

Then the past comes heaving back
in unwanted names and circumstances
that clearcut his senses,
and the words turn to spittle
in the cracked corners of his mouth:
"He sailed" is past tense.

The Right Slope

Wanting to mount the right slope
in the right season of life,
he walked deep into his blood
and furrowed there for seeds
even as winter ripped at his flesh.

Before he had listened too deep,
the greentime was on him,
past, and left him holding dried seed
in a new depth of cold
even as the sun burned his flesh.

He had not gone deep enough
to be allowed to climb.

Along Denton Road – September

The lake today was empty–
whole bays boatless,
whole waves untouched by hulls or oars,
the air unsounded by engines.

A bright orange crowned certain maples,
early Cassandras
that the chill air was pregnant
with storm, snow and cold.

I walked my nightly way
along dirt of Denton Road,
above the lake, led by a wind
that came off the waves
with the smell of fall water.

The hunger came like a sudden windshift.
As often as I touch,
the touch shrinks me
when underneath the flesh is flame,
wanting the heat of close bodies,
the touch of friends,
their breaths, their raucous laughs,
their quiet presence
beside the same remembered scenes,
wanting the heat of a lover
sharing the sweat and the bed
and the intense echo of the pulse
in the ears and in the eyes
as we lie together after.

I walk in the delicious cold
as the sun splays along the land
and stretches long shadows
from the clouds and between the trees.

I know how cold this death is.
I welcome it. The hunger.
Always unsatisfied, always striding
down the dirt road with my head
thrown back and my mouth open
to catch the air and the sky,
the low clouds bobbing
with my every impatient step.
I accept the hunger and fear it.
It has no end except in ends.
It has no satisfaction
no matter how intense the friendship,
no matter how damp the after breathing
with any lover.

The empty lake lay open
to the long lights of a full sunset.
It might seem satisfied
if a lake could be animated.
But the soul of any scene
of any color of any wind
is the soul the self provides it.
I am hungry, and the countryside
should wear my soul.
Instead the empty lake mirrors
the pasteled sky and the close clouds
and the perfect roll of the process,
no season, no day. no hour,
no marking post, no decision, no desire.

I find my self evaporating
into my stride, the dancing up
and down of the darkening sky,
my walk elongating into cast light,
my desire dissipating into cast shadow.

The empty waves that roll from bank to bank
don't move water with their movement
but toss it up and down
and leave it all behind.

The wave moves across the river,
but the water ignores the wave
except to rise and fall when it passes.
And so the wave doesn't exist.

I bob up and down in the motion
of my walking home tonight.
The sky moves up and down with me.
We are each unmoved,
like the water being waved.
I am the wave, the figmentary motion
that does not exist
but merely moves the sky, the clouds,
the trees, with openmouthed walking.

And the fragmentary motion
of the season, of the sky,
of my self down Denton Road
I ignore, emptied like the lake
when the dam's sluices are ungated,
ready to put an end to seasons,
hungers, satisfactions,
ready to stretch myself out
like and elongating shadow
until the shadow meets the night
in markless completion,
in full measure of desireless want,
in the darkness when the clouds disappear
or are merely the absence of some stars.

Kensington Lake Walk

One bedraggled red-tail hawk,
stark in bare-branched oak
against gray January–

Three woodpeckers:
one downy,
one red-headed,
one hairy–

Two tufted titmice–

Six or so white-breasted
nuthatches walking
heads downwards along
the beech and aspen,
pecking the cold bark for food–

Three gray squirrels
and two fox squirrels–

Two yearlings and a doe,
pawing the ground,
gnawing tree bark–

Dozens of black-capped
chickadees, gregarious
little preachers in the branches
overhead– all chattering,
scolding, lecturing–

except the one that braves
the palm of my hand
to take black sunflower seeds
into a tree, clutching each
between talons,
breaking open with chopping

motions of his head,
billing out the soft kernels within–

confident that
neither this winter
nor my hand
will close about him.

Beneath the Dreaming Trees

Beneath the dreaming trees
in the silence of mist morning
while silver frost reaped limbs
to brown ground gleaning,
the stranger walked unknowing
into the crunch of glint-tipped leaves.

The color clattered beneath his feet
 in measure with his smoking breath.
Gray scents of hard dawnlight
licked the edge of eastern trees
as he halted, as frozen as
the crystals in gray steel grass.

Behind him night retreated
into the shadows he'd crushed
with his fleeing feet in silvered earth.
He sat in the brown and silver
noise of leaves, his back
to the blueblack ebbing darkness.

He heard the last of frost
exhaling from the leaves into the sun
now loud above him. Only then
did he raise his eyes from leaping shadows.
Only then, his frost eyes melted
and his flesh crumbled into leaves

as his breath entered the clouds
that rose steaming from the hills.

Dust of the Mundane

Clouds dressed and undressed the sky all day,
shadows straying across fields and dirt roads.
I walked against the traffic of the clouds,
they streaming east down the dry highway,
echoed by shadows and by dust-arousing
cars. I walked their windblown dust.
Soon my feet itched where they met
the shoes because, sockless, I had come
to wear brown leggings of sweat-streaked dust.
As the clouds have abandoned all hope
of making their endless goal before
the night dissolves them into white stars,
so I have given up the desire of reaching
my home before dissolving into the road dust.
And so I walk easily against the traffic
of the clouds, dust, and cars, humming quietly.

Wearing the Abyss

"When you look too long into an abyss,
the abyss looks into you." – *Nietzsche*

I am become
hurricane,
whirling manifestation
of the abyss
I too long
look into.
I wear whorls
in my bloodstream.
I hear winds
in my earpulse.
I am made of water
and wild air.
In the end, I
dissipate across
the wide plains
in rain,
brief flashes,
and long echoes.

Water-Walker

The water walker dances
his ripples on the surface
tension of the pond
across its smooth reflectivity.

Beneath, on brown pond
bottom,
a long-legged shadow
spider hops in echo.

In the water, rhythmed
to the water-walker's stride,
a swaying miniature of sun
shines up from pond sky.

For an hour
I sit beside the pond,
occasionally sucked by
a mosquito,

occasionally observed by
a forest bird or ground squirrel.
And I measure---
for an hour---

the distance from the walker
to his shadow,
the distance of his shadow
from the sun.

Eyelight and Crawfish Questions

It isn't enough to see the whirl,
the ripples and the eddies
and the reflections of light
dancing fairy above the water.
Nor is it something special
to become the water,
to find the eye and mind
waved within the creek
and the evanescence of water
flowing the is and is not.
Surely the crawfish and brook trout
have superior knowledge
if seeing and being within the water
is the definition of wisdom.
To recognize that the whirl,
the ripples, the eddies, and the refraction
are truth and essence of it all
may be nearer the mark.
And then, to find the patternless
pattern both within the whirl and oneself.
To recognize the shape in the ear
and ripple as a wave against eardrum
called sound--and the eddy of the stream
echoed in the eddy in the heart,
hesitant between beats--called life,
and reflection of fairy light
an illusion of flesh and photons
against the retina--this may be yet
more the way of knowledge.
Still, it is incomplete.
No, complete it is, in fact.
Rather, it is insufficient
to the whole notion of creek,
to the philosophy of water,
to the science of sun near setting.
To recognize the mutual making

in the placement of the creek,
the sun, the light, the watching self
is truer than the disconnected nature
of earlier explanation.
The mutual making is, however,
not of separate things at all.
It is not that I have relationship
with creek, crawfish, and light.
Rather it is that I am relation
mutually done, and that the creek
and I would not be, or would be other
if the mutuality were not.
It would be a different creek.
It would be different eyes.
I would be a different seer
if the creek chose else
to be created in the seeing.
No. That's still not it.
That's closer. But still not it.
Perhaps in another decade of trying,
another life of looking,
another creek, another crawfish,
I will be present when words
fall right, and a world is born.
And then it is enough to be and see
whirling eddies, crawfish light.

Wisdom of the Common Grackle

He was instructed by the suddenness
of grackles shot from the grass
in black wings and green fluorescence.

What could he learn that he had not
already ignored? Yellow beads of eyes.
Bird shrieks. The bare treelimbs.

He wore the sky in his eyes, except
that he could not see it there.
He saw instead the lead colored clouds.

Shivering, he breathed in cold
January, held it inside against
his ribs, and let it free in breath-smoke.

Learning. The birds for leaves
in the barren trees. Evergreens
full of bird voices, not meaning anything.

Mind wordless for the microsecond
of his seeing, he took his lessons
seriously, and made his blood understand.

Or he forgot. In dropping sky,
snow downing, crystals melting
on his upturned face. Forgetting.

He was the memory of what needed
him. Sky lowering. Trees singing
in the sway, full-bird voiced.

Enough. Be wordless in the space
that follows. Instantness of grackle.
Gray sky. Evergreen bending over. Snow.

Bead

Jeweled in water death,
he watched as the sea
beaded to life on his body,
quickened, ran in rivers,
spilled back, and declined
to become a man spirit.

The spell fell down to him
who was the weakest,
and bent him straight
for a drowned horizon.
He sang the water death,
and the water reborn.

Facing Olympus

With age should come wisdom,
and yet, here am I, a graybeard,

half as wise as when I was twenty.
Like Lear, I have raged against

the hurricane, but am not yet
mad. How quickly the kingdom

of my youth has passed away.
I own more now. I have title,

and land, and enough wealth
to be comfortable for a while.

The young man in me, in my memory,
reminds me that I have cashed in

dreams to make that comfort.
Old men are too comfortable.

Old men need to face the precipice,
stand against the wind, recall

the courage of youth, and then
in the madness of the hurricane,

come face to face with wisdom—
the unutterable One— and, wearing

Muses horns, descend to a last valley
with a dazed smile and pure white hair.

Shades of Gray

The muscles tightened in his thighs
like bands of fingers clutching the bone,
as he climbed the tall hill, sidestepping
to keep from tumbling backwards

down towards the river in the valley.
He felt the drumming of his heart
against the cage of bone in his chest,
and the slow burning in his throat,

as if he'd drunk warm brandy.
The brown clutter of dry leaves crackled
and dry branches snapped, echoing
through the fall-barrened woods:

Undergrowth shed to thin sticks
and arches of branches with few,
rattling leaves in the valley wind.
At the crest of the ridge, he paused,

eyed the steep hillside, and saw,
far below near the bend in the river,
a figure looking back up at him.
He could not tell the age or sex.

Just a dim figure studying his climb.
He began to raise his hand to wave,
when suddenly the figure took the form
of a split treetrunk, cracked limbs

jutting out for arms, and a gnarled knot
near the jagged top he'd taken for a hat.
Self-conscious of his half-raised hand,
he brought it back against his body.

The woods were empty. No animal stirred.
No bird dashed from tree to tree.
No leaves pirouetted---there was no wind.
The drumming of his heart stilled.

His need had metamorphosed oak
to the visage of his Shadow self.
How could his need transform the sky
which dropped in shades of gray to dusk?

Oregon Redream

He remembered suddenly,
stood from his long somnolence
and began to seek the roadway.
The map was stained, outdated,
word, seams split through
from refolding folds unfolding.
Some of the writing
had eroded. Some
of the places named
no longer existed.
But it was what he had.

As he had laid it out
new on the cliffedge
in Oregon, and there lost it,
he thought forever,
he did not understands now
how it had reappeared
in his hip pocket
thirty-four years later
and older that he ever
thought he could be.

He took its appearance
on faith, and sought
the roadway or trail
that would reach the summit,
the one he had failed
to reach because July
was still rich deep in hard snow,
the summit where water
is pure, clean, cold, potable,
where the snowmelt
sourced into a young spirit,
Where the evergreen
predominate and night sky

is black with hard steady stars
piercing through to heaven.

The map was present,
tangible, but incomprehensible.
His rusted compass wavered
across the four cardinal
directions while his pulse
raced like an old man's
in a dream of recalled youth.
He started awake, disappointed
to find his empty hands,
the map still lost to degrading
in an old Oregon, awake
to find his years run out
with only dust in his mouth
instead of song.

Somehow he took it on faith
that the map had spoken.
And he crawled from bed
to a new day with
the quietest scent of pine
and campfire ash in his nostrils.

Sparrow Flight

A walk in mud made me
return with this December
to bright fire in trees.

I can resurrect light
with the sound of sawing
scent of evergreen from sawdust.

No new snow, mere old snow
transfigured to mire
that holds me dear to earth

Where I have one place
before nightfall, one door
to open hearth home.

Absences redeem time
from stale photographs,
return me from nostalgia

to that one place nowed
in the blood of this season,
having birthed me six

Decades ago from nothing
sparrow flight through warm
light to the acheless winter.

The scars remain in soil,
on my knee, my knuckles,
my jut of jaw and thrust

Of making from decay
the mulch of meaning
springing April greening.

The vacant echo steps
the final sidewalk concrete
to the flick of fire,

Real arms to embrace
and take my winter cloak
from me, my birthright

This month of long nights,
cold days, holy days spent
in that sparrow hall, singing.

Coda: The Geese Wait Upriver

The V of Canada geese slide
downward, then un-V and, single file,
glide into the water, sledding
white sprays of water
like silver snow outward.

Behind me, the young boy walks,
perhaps a half-mile away,
falling farther and farther behind.
He stops often to toss a stone
at the water, wanting so much
that his ripple circle-making
carry the world over.
After each bend, I try to wait
for him to catch up, but finally
have to walk onward downstream.
Each time he turns the bend himself,
he gets harder and harder
to see. He seems to shrink up
into the green willows that lean
over the water, dangling branches
into the current as the boy
would dangle a fishing line.

The geese have hunkered down
for the night as the sun
leans upriver. They preen
and fluff feathers, nesting
themselves into the reeds and weed
along the shoreline near sunset water.
They cackle their evening
gaggle-talk, sliding into darkness
with a friendly communion.

Ahead of me, around the curve
of the river path,

I keep catching glimpses
of the old man.
He may be the boy's grandfather,
pausing regularly, waiting out
the boy's playful explorations
until he comes home.
His gray hair and beard,
his vulture stoop at the shoulders,
his steady but slow stride,
rising like a farmer
to step across the furrows.
At each bend in the river,
I see more of him.
Steadily, I am catching up.

I worry about the boy since
I can no longer see him
in the redefining dusk.

It is a quiet sunset.
And the geese are out of the sky.

Epilogue

Rock, Paper, Scissors

Prelude

Rock, paper, scissors.
Throw the hands, see who wins,
something wins, someone always
cuts, breaks, covers.

On the streetcorner,
in the alley, hands behind,
counting, one, two, three,
see–someone wins,
someone always
cuts, breaks, covers.

Rock breaks Scissors

Design images and place
them carefully in patterns.
Arrange the patterns.
Analyze the arrangements.

And still the cat corpse
rotting on the roadside.
And still the break of branch
in a wild dark wind.

And still the encroaching
fat around the waist,
the lessening breath,
the graying of the hair and flesh.

Understanding breaks
against such things.
Death resists designs,
denies our analysis.

Crushed chest to steering wheel.
He was broken against
the curve of the highway,
his life foaming on his lips,

despite the careful design
of yellow lines on pavement.
The highway accepted
with the stoicism of stone.

A heart collapses on
a dance floor,
despite the careful
arrangement of steps.

She fades like dyed cloth
in the sunmost window,
despite the careful arrangement
of her long, red hair,

the long withering of her
crisp and comprehensive gaze into
age and uncomprehending stare.
The breaking of mind against these things.

Stone breaks scissors.
Stone breaks mind and tissue.
And still, as hard as stone:
the knowledge of the unredeemed

rock of the body and
the breaking of the breath
and blood against
the eventual hardness of our dark.

Scissors Cut Paper

Try to hide the scissors cuts
along the wrists and forearms,
like pinpricks of an addict's

needle   try to hide the
serrations of the cut cloth
of flesh. Try to hide.

Think, and the world forgets
you, and you forget the world.
Think is enemy to things.

Suddenly, the words fell home,
the heartbeat triumphed,
the edge was danced
without the slice of blade
severing flesh from speech.
See, it can be done.

But when the voice is tried
against the conceit of paper,
the eye says Things,
and the mind responds
with terrible silence
and a thousand voices
worrying the words.

The flesh forms a scar.
It has been severed
after the fact, and is mended
only by nerveless tissue,
pale gray instead of pink,
and numb to the touch.

Logically, there are only
two choices. Logically.
(1) You can choose between
two choices. Or, (2),
you can refuse to choose.
Scissors and paper. Scissors
and stones make fragments of us all.

Enough. With the same scissors
you can dance the edge

of blade on blade, not
choosing, deciding only
when the paper separates,
each fiber severed, each
piece whole and distinct,
but the whole category,
paper, still preserved, still
whole, still, finally, just paper.

Paper Covers Rock

Too much paper, too many words.
Try to cover the world
with inked paper.
Waste of paper.
Roxanne in the treeleaves.
Rice paper poems in
the wind, underfoot.
Books burned in Alexandria,
in Rome, in Berlin.
Ashes in the wind,
and underfoot.
The woodpulp of a hundred
thousand forests feeds
the presses which squeeze
out ink like blood
from the winepress
onto the flesh of the paper,
too much paper, words.

Sometimes when the moon
is full, or isn't, when
the rhythm in the blood
matches the wrist to the flow
of ink on white paper
sometimes, paper redeems.
Not the words or the phrases,
not the literal paper itself,
in its unmended fibers.
No, the idea of paper

and the images on paper
sometimes melt the world.
What then? Melt the world
and paper burns like libraries.
Fanatics use words too.
What then?

Rock, Paper, Scissors

Rock, Paper, Scissors.
In the end, everything
is covered, cut, broken.
We separate with metal.
We break against rock.
We try to mend with words
and bits of paper.

Her eyes glazed over,
and became gray steel.
His heart siezed up,
and became an iron rock.

Take the sheets of paper
from the broken ream
and cover them, cover
them with words.

In the end, everything
is blown away by wind,
everything melts in rain,
and everything is bare.

Not covered. Paper
cannot cover stone.
Paper cannot mend with scissors.
Paper melts in rain, poor flesh.

In the end, everything
is cut, broken, uncovered.
We stand with fractured

scissors, a lump of stone
in our throats, watching
the paper of our lives
drift across the parking lot,
a white scudding before
the knife of wind
across the darkest stone.

Coda

Rock, Paper, Scissors.
The hands balance between
throws. One, two, three.
See, something always,
someone always, cuts,
breaks, covers–always.

In the balance between
throws, the trialectic
holds. What are scissors
without paper to cleave?
What is a stone without
scissors to break?

What is paper without the
rock to redeem in white
and ink/blood, in the balance
between throws? But this
between balances forever
in that moment.

Hands must throw.
Someone must win.
Something always
cuts, breaks, covers.
The balance is overthrown again,
and hands return behind.

Sculpting in Clay

All those sunsets forge him
down, thrust towards a new
shape. In his combined vectors,
results are less than mathematical
and more than simply flowing.

From drawings past
the artist forces out
the growths of god. Or,
less creates, but more than
awaits a clayshape for his soul
that takes it all higher than
reflected light can understand him.

Time shapes for any man,
then wheels itself in shiny
skin, wriggling snakelife
thru the weeds after
its own rattle.
Dust rejoins the river,
drags him undertowed with it,
beaches him on a stray
island, too late for morning.

All those set suns blind
early eyes, remain in
retinal afterimage to blue
dim dots at the forehead center.
In him combined, more
simply flowing, more hushed,
more timed, the serpentine
slide of his carving.

For Linda: Near Gatlinburg, March 2006

Sitting on that sun-warmed rock,
its slate broken by time and
smoothed by rushing water,
you smile into cold sunshine.

In that smile, I see the younger
woman you say you used to be.
I see you as a steady stream,
like this river from the Appalachians,

always flowing towards the Gulf,
always bringing cold mountains
down towards the warm seas,
always certain in my wayward stream.

I Am of Appalachians

I am of Appalachians, old
mountains worn round and green
by millennia of wind and water.

Born of Pennsylvania red clay
and hilltops of black loam,
slate and sandstone and hard-faced

cuts made by men to highway through
passes, I breathed coaldust, played
with the bright glass in rough slag,

and skipped red dog across creeks,
cutting hands and knees so the
crystals from old smelt became

my flesh, invisible clarity of
ache glistening in the right light.
My dreams still flow of muddy

Youghiogheny water. Neither
the flat Michigan plains of gray clay
and brown sand nor the white dunes

of Northern Florida filled with palms,
bright azalea beside blue ocean
can displace the green mountains

that enfold the creases of my brain,
holograms of a youth of living slant
on the side ways of the hills.

Remountained now to Virginia
and horizons of the Blue Ridge,
I am becoming as old as Appalachian

mountains, as hungry as cataracts
and roaring creeks sluicing down
mountain sides of spring melt.

In my end, I return to what had
made me, become as hard and black
as anthracite, residual of all organic,

latent of the all consuming fire
to make me glassy slag entire,
brilliant in the remnants of the hills.

Acknowledgements

Many are owed my gratitude, and I fear leaving some out. My senior high school English teacher, Doris Roe, taught me how to be a ruthless editor of my own writing. Ron English encouraged my writing when I was a fumbling college student. Bill Shuter was a dear friend and always read my attempts at poetry with respect and interest. Fellow writers including Betty Stover and William R. Allen supported my early efforts and Richard Dine helped me print my own chapbook, *Dark Land, White Light*.

Patrick Bradley has been vital in helping me compile and edit poetry from across four decades. His enthusiasm and interest and that of Cheryl Huff have helped me greatly. Allan Peterson encouraged me to begin writing again after a long hiatus and always asks just the right question to encourage me to find the better word or phrase.

The impact of my now lost parents, Tony and Ann, cannot be explained, thanked, or fully expressed.

My family and especially Linda deserve the highest gratitude for their love and support. Linda, thank you for being beside me always, and thank you for reading my writing and letting me know what you think, no matter what. You are priceless.

"Bend, Oregon: July "originally published as "Oregon, 1972" in *The FreeLance*

"Fatherhood" originally published in the *Wayne Review*

About the author:

David Anthony Sam was born and spent his childhood in McKeesport PA, a coal and steel suburb of Pittsburgh. His home at the end of 36th Street abutted a woods, and the games he played on that street and the time he spent in those woods all influenced his poetry as well as his sense of the holistic ecology of all things. His neighborhood was filled with immigrants and children of immigrants, and his grandparents themselves came from Poland and Syria.

In 1961, the family moved with his father's factory to Belleville, MI, a far suburb of Detroit. Small town life near a lake and the rural farm fields and woods within a short walk along the railroad tracks also appear in this volume of semiautobiographical verse.

A first-generation college student and graduate of Eastern Michigan University and Michigan State University, Sam has taught creative writing, English literature, and composition at Eastern Michigan, Marygrove College, Oakland Community College, and Pensacola State College. He was partner/manager of Gondolier Music & Electronics from 1972-1985 in Belleville before moving into higher education as an administrator.

With his wife and life partner, Linda, he lives now in Culpeper VA, still within sight of the eastern mountain chain. They have two children, Michelle and Ryan, and four grandchildren. Sam serves as president of Germanna Community College and persists in writing poetry.

Made in the USA
San Bernardino, CA
12 May 2014